Life in Christ

Life in Christ

A call to be in His Presence

With every Blessing,
Mary Fleeson

LINDISFARNE
SCRIPTORIUM

Mary Fleeson

This first edition published by:
Lindisfarne Scriptorium Limited,
Farne House, Marygate,
Holy Island of Lindisfarne,
TD15 2SJ, United Kingdom.
www.lindisfarne-scriptorium.co.uk

ISBN-13: 978 0 9561402 1 0

10 9 8 7 6 5 4 3 2 1

Text acknowledgements:

'Christ has no body now but yours' prayer, words attributed to Theresa of Avila copyright unknown.
Scripture quotations taken from the Holy Bible, NIV and NKJV translation.

British Library Cataloguing in Publication Data. A catalogue record for this book is available from the British Library.

Typeset by Lindisfarne Scriptorium Limited.
Book production and preparation by Burning Light Solutions Limited.
Printed and bound in China.

This book is dedicated to my amazing family. Mark, my husband and my rock.
Aurian and Calum, my precious children.
And the very youthful Aged Parents, both sets!

Contents

Foreword

by David Fitzgerald, Musician, Teacher and co-founder of the band Iona.

Invitation

Chapters

Foreword

For as long as I can remember there are two things that have been central to my life: art and music. I have to say that it was music that spoke to me first and that remains so. In my youngest days I began also to appreciate art and literature and these became all the more important and influential once I was introduced to the Christian faith. It was through the painting 'The Light Of The World' by Holman Hunt that I was to discover the Saviour of the World and of my life. This picture is based upon a verse from the New Testament: 'Behold, I stand at the door and knock. If anyone hears my voice and opens the door, I will come in to him and dine with him, and he with me' (Revelation 3:20 NKJV). As the painting was explained to me I saw very clearly that Christ was standing outside the door of my heart (and of my life) and that if this door was ever going to be opened it was going to have to be opened by me (the handle of the door is on the inside). There are so many symbols in this painting and all of them based upon Scripture. The central theme is the Man with the lantern - He is Christ who brings Light to the world. It is an amazing painting and makes a profound impression upon me each time I encounter it. (I have seen two of the originals a number of times – in St Paul's Cathedral, in Manchester's City Art Gallery and again at the incredible Millennium exhibition at the National Gallery in London entitled 'Seeing Salvation – The Image Of Christ').

As I have journeyed through life other amazing discoveries have been made, most of these quite unexpected – they have been introduced to me 'out of the blue' it would seem! I know now that these have been sacred moments and that God has used art and symbols to show me something so amazingly special. These have gone on to be used to speak to and inspire me (and my friends and colleagues) to express and to interpret them into sound. One thing I do know is that without the eyes of faith I would not have seen or understood all that the artist was seeking to convey to me. When I initially encountered The Book Of Kells it was like an explosion in my senses! I first discovered this amazing ancient Celtic treasure in a bookshop in Glastonbury. As I turned the pages my spirit rose and I began to hear sounds as the colours and symbols seemed to leap out and immerse me within another world. Years later I was to discover another amazing book, entitled 'Life Journey' by Mary Fleeson. Here the colours, intricate art and calligraphy are made all the more powerful as each theme is entwined with powerful text (this time in contemporary English – so that I could understand!). Once again sounds began to accompany word and image as I explored each page.

I am so very privileged to have got to know Mary, husband Mark and their dear children Aurian and Calum. They have become good friends and an inspiration to me over the years. Living and working on the Holy Island of Lindisfarne has been for them life changing.

Those who have made the journey across the causeway from the mainland and visited the island will know that you never leave this sacred space the same. You will have been deeply touched by the powerful beauty of its landscape, the sounds around you and even more by the presence of God. This place is saturated by centuries of prayer and evangelism by saints such as Aidan, Cuthbert and Bishop Eadfrith (author of the magnificent Lindisfarne Gospels). Their lives and many others across the years have been offered up to God in a life of devotion, love and sacrifice.

Centuries later many people are drawn to this place. Some have chosen to settle and to live there and to become a part of the island's community and legacy. The work of Mary (her 'Opus Dei') is a continuation of what has taken place since Irish monks from the Island of Iona first settled on Lindisfarne and established their monastery.

For me, as a musician who has been deeply impressed and inspired by the landscape, presence, writings and art from Holy Island, it has been both wonderful and amazing to be profoundly inspired by the contemporary work of Mary and to know that her work is intrinsically woven in to all that has come before. What is all the more exciting is that her art and text is a part of a world that we all inhabit right now. Mary's beautiful images are indeed something more - a reflection of past, present and future. They speak to me of two worlds - a world within a world – and of the eternal particularly. As you explore the pages of this book you will discover, again and again, that our journey into God is continuous, always fresh and (as Mary has expressed it) 'a little scary as well as amazing'!
Wherever you might find yourself in the journey it is reassuring to know that 'everyone has a golden Christ-shaped void in them, where He lives already', invited at the very moment that a person has said to Him 'please Lord, do come in'. We are never alone.

I thank God that through the power and the beauty of art my life has been profoundly changed, again and again over the years.

May this book inspire you, as you move through each theme, and be of help to you in the journey. May these words and beautiful images assist you to discover the skills and the gifts that God has already placed within you and to use these for His glory and for the service of those waiting to be blessed by them.

David Fitzgerald - January 2009
Musician, Teacher and co-founder of the band Iona.

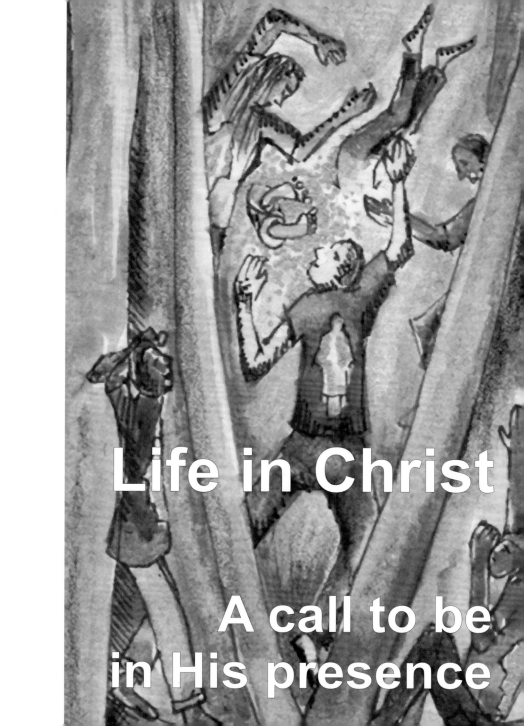

Life in Christ

A call to be in His presence

Forever

That He may live in us and we in Him,
The idea is amazing.
That I might rest, cradled in His arms,
Hold His hand, look at my God and say
I love You,
And
Hear Him say the same.
That through the wine and bread,
A simple meal yet complex in the taking,
I might invite His presence inside
And dwell in him forever.

Welcome...

...to this, my second book. If you are familiar with the first book, 'Life Journey - A call to Christ-centred living', then you will find that this can be used in the same way, as an individual or in a small group.

Each chapter contains original poetry, meditation and prayer and in most cases Bible references, activities and design notes, to accompany the artwork.

'Life in Christ' is a continuation of a Christ-centred journey, its aim is to encourage you to be in His presence constantly, not only leading a life centred in Him but also, as the advert used to say, to learn how to 'work, rest and play', in Him.

As in 'Life Journey', this is not a book of answers, it is the musing of an ordinary person travelling a well trodden path, trying not to trip over the stones or fall over the cliff at the side. Sometimes the path goes uphill and I hope that this book will be a helping hand. Sometimes the path will be easy, take time to enjoy the details!

That he may Live in us and we in him

Design notes

This piece draws words from an Eucharist service. The concept has always excited me, the idea that Jesus, God, is more than just beside me and all around me but that He is inside me, is amazing. His holy and perfect Spirit is enmeshed with my sinful and not-so-perfect spirit. Also the idea that He wants us to be so secure in His presence that we are living continually in His company is a little scary as well as amazing.

For the design I wanted to show ordinary people being in God's presence. Jesus is more than life size in comparison to the people around Him to show His Godhead and he looks down to where his heart is open and people are invited to enter. The people are at different stages of their journey with Christ, some are struggling to hold on to the hem of his robe, trying to understand and desperately wanting to know more; some are diving into His heart, ready to give themselves completely; some are happy to be where they are for now; some scared to go further. Everyone has a golden Christ-shaped void in them where He lives already, invited to be there at the very moment a person sought Him.

Take the skills I have Lord, and make them Your own.

Take the gifts I have and bless their use,

Grant me opportunities to try new things

And the courage to make a mess of them.

A Call to Beginning

Chapter One

IN THE BEGINNING WAS the WORD, AND the WORD was with GOD, AND the WORD was GOD. 2 The same was in the BEGINNING WITH GOD. 3 ALL THINGS WERE made by HIM; and WITHOUT him was not ANYTHING MADE that was MADE. 4 IN HIM was LIFE; and the LIFE was the LIGHT of MEN. 5 AND LIGHT SHINeth in DARKNESS; AND the DARKness COMPREHENDeD IT NOT.

TO THE GLORY OF GOD ALONE   MARY FLEESON 2001

John Chapter One

In the beginning was the Word,
and the Word was with God,
and the Word was God.
The same was in the beginning with God.
All things were made by him;
and without him was not any thing made that was made.
In him was life; and the life was the light of men.
And the light shineth in darkness;
and the darkness comprehended it not.

The Light of the World

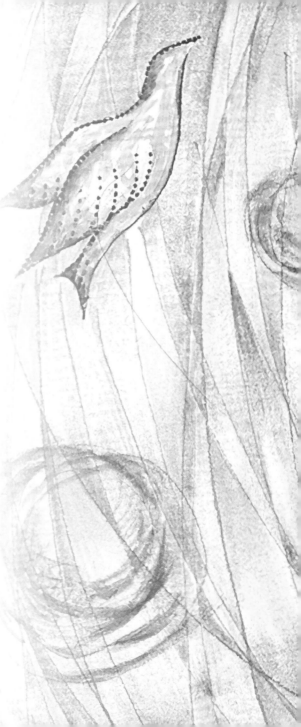

The light has come into the world,
      The voice boomed out amidst the cathedral stones
But men loved the darkness rather than the light.
      He reaches out, an attempt to offer love.
Bang. The drum beats loudly.
      The human heart which spews forth sin.
          Bang. Bang.
          Change us.
          Bang. Bang.
He climbs the steps.
      Willingly.
          Bang. Bang.
Nails pierce.
      The beat reverberates around the holy pillars.
          Bang. Bang.
It echoes from the shadowed roof.
      He dies.
          Lament.
A light shines on a figure rising.

The light shines in the darkness,
And the darkness has never put it out.

16

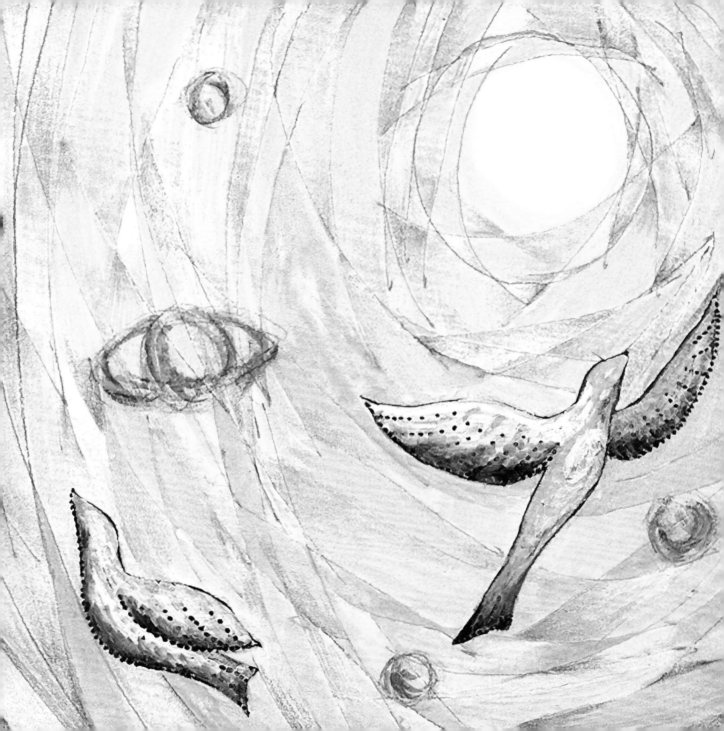

Meditation

I love starting something new, a fresh notepad, a new pack of cereals, a box of paints, an unread book, I always feel a sense of anticipation at the possibilities, excitement at the new opportunities, sheer pleasure at the freshness – I know, that's all a bit over the top for a packet of cornflakes but strangely it's true! Imagine God's delight at His new world, all shiny and perfect in every way.

Imagine His sadness when His greatest, most beloved creation turns away from Him. It would be like me finding moths in my cornflakes or someone else's scribble three pages into my new notepad, but much, much worse.

When we become Christians we are made new, we have a greater awareness of the sins that we have been forgiven for and God can write on our clean hearts His vision for our lives in His presence. This world will one day be made new again, the process has begun and it continues with you and every person who seeks and meets Christ.

Design notes

This piece depicts aspects of creation, plants, animals, birds and the cosmos against the background of a view of Holy Island seen from the causeway.

Activity

Is there anything in your life that needs beginning again?

Anything which needs to be made new?

Write these things down and offer them as a prayer.

Prayer

Expose the dark corners of my heart Lord,
Fill them with light.
May I no longer find safety hiding in the shadows.

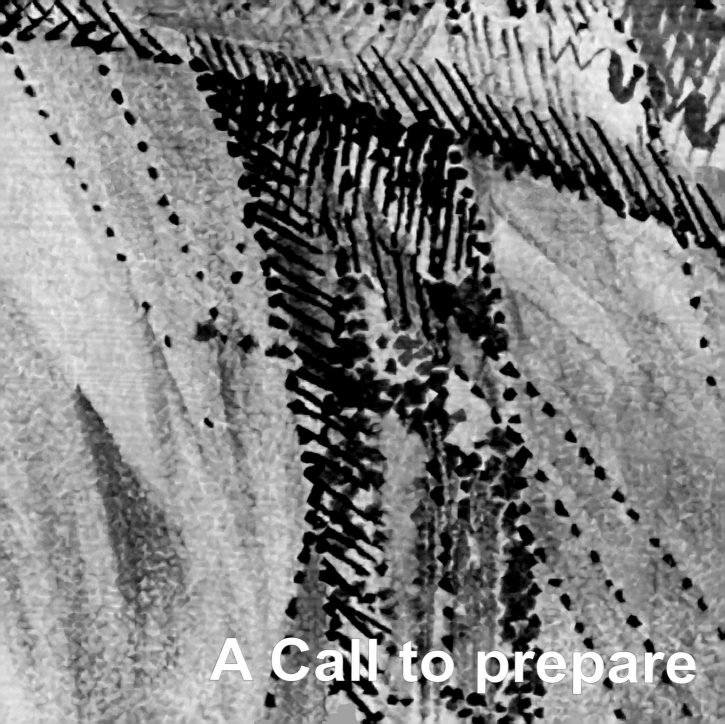

A Call to prepare

I BIND MY MIND
TO THE MIND OF THE CREAT...
THAT I MAY WORSHIP COMPLETEL...
I BIND MY BODY
TO THE WILL OF THE SAVIO...
THAT I MAY SERVE FREELY
I BIND MY SPIRIT
TO THE HOLY SPIRIT HEL...
THAT I MAY LOVE JOYFULLY

AND LOOSE FROM MY MIND ALL THAT OFFENDS MY GOD

AND LOOSE FROM MY BODY ALL DIS-EASE

AND LOOSE FROM MY SPIRIT ALL THAT IS NOT OF MY GOD

Trinity

I bind my mind to the mind
of the Creator God
and I loose from my mind
all that offends my God.
That I may worship completely.

I bind my body to the will
of the Saviour Christ
and I loose from my body
all dis-ease.
That I may serve Freely.

I bind my spirit to the Holy Spirit
my helper
and I loose from my spirit
all that is not of my God.
That I may love joyfully...

Hope

We cling to the masts,
Our boats are battered and turned around and around,
Shaken and threatened.
Our cries are lost in the cries of the world,
Our tears only add to the swelling of grief.
Overwhelming sadness,
Compassion-free lives challenged by hope.
Fear of tomorrow confronted by love.
We need not drown,
Our boat is strong, the mast is secure.
The Spirit within us makes us buoyant.
Reach out, hold on
....hope to change the world.

Meditation

Binding and loosing is a prayer technique often used in terms of spiritual warfare, the enemy can be bound and rendered impotent by a prayer said with accurate discernment and in the name of Jesus.

The Trinity prayer is more personal, it prepares us for battle by aligning us with the Holy Spirit in our mind, body and soul. Binding ourselves to God is like tying ourselves to the mast of a strong boat in a storm, we may not be in control but we won't get washed overboard or drowned by life's storms. The loosing aspect involves releasing things (wrong emotions, attitudes, relationships) from our spirit so that the enemy cannot use them as a foothold and make us ineffective as Christians and as human beings.

Knowing that we have done as much as we can to prepare ourselves for battle reinforces the hope we have in the resurrection. The battle has been won but if we want to be effective disciples then our call is to fight for the souls not yet won and a world not yet made perfect.

Matthew 18:18 "I tell you the truth, whatever you **bind on earth** will be **bound in heaven**, and whatever you **loose on earth** will be **loosed in heaven**."

Ephesians 6:13-18 Therefore put on the full armour of God, so that when the day of evil comes, you may be able to stand your ground, and after you have done everything, to stand. Stand firm then, with the belt of truth buckled around your waist, with the breastplate of righteousness in place, and with your feet fitted with the readiness that comes from the gospel of peace. In addition to all this, take up the shield of faith, with which you can extinguish all the flaming arrows of the evil one. Take the helmet of salvation and the sword of the Spirit, which is the word of God. And pray in the Spirit on all occasions with all kinds of prayers and requests.

Prayer

My God, my Saviour, my Helper,
My strength and my provider,
I need You more each moment,
I need You deeper every day.
My soul cries out - comfort me my Lord.
My mind seeks wisdom - teach me Lord.
My body is weak - help me Lord.

A Call to Love

Love Is

Love is always patient and kind.
Love is not boastful or conceited.
It is never rude, and never seeks its own advantage.
It does not take offence or store up grievances.
Love does not rejoice in wrong doing but finds its joy in the truth.
It is always ready to make allowances, to trust,
to hope and to endure whatever comes.
These remain: faith, hope and love, and the greatest is love.

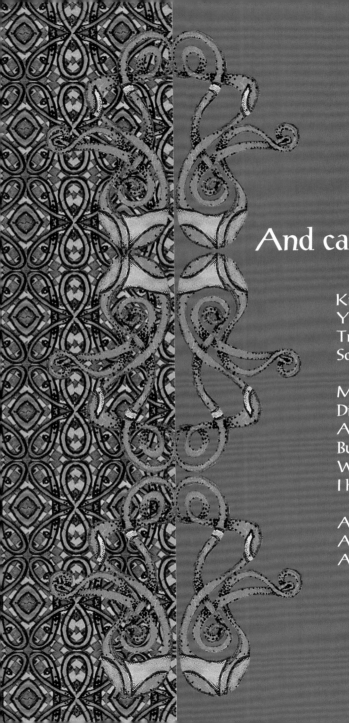

And can sin be redeemed?

Kind? Patient?
Yes, I'm all that and so modest you'll find.
Truth versus lies?
Sometimes the latter is so much more kind.

Manners maketh a human so I've heard,
Disrespect is a mask,
A cruel action, a cruel word,
But I can cope if you're rude to me,
We're all the same don't you see,
I hurt you, and you hurt me.

And can hope survive the pain?
And can trust outlive a broken heart?
And can sin be redeemed by love?

Meditation

1 Corinthians, chapter 13 is probably the most popular Bible passage chosen to read at weddings, it's words are read to remind the happy couple what the foundation of marriage should be, and the congregation what the foundation of life itself should be. The words tell us that love is at the root of living in community with each other and in harmony with God, it will be the only thing that will remain when everything else has gone.

Whilst having many meanings, the word love is used in the Bible with great power,

Jesus said,
"A new command I give you: Love one another. As I have loved you, so you must love one another."

and

"For God so loved the world that he gave his one and only Son, that whoever believes in him shall not perish but have eternal life."

The kind of love Jesus spoke about was completely unconditional, self-sacrificing and pure. Many people today use the word 'love' with the same kind of disregard as they cry out to God when they really want to say "Wow isn't that amazing / awful / shocking / gorgeous!".

If we could communicate the power of love (without using cheesy pop songs) we could share the mind-blowing possibilities of a world where love is the first thought and the first action.

Activity

Ask yourself,

Am I patient, am I kind? Do I
envy, do I boast, am I proud?

Am I rude, am I self-seeking,
am I easily angered, do I keep
a record of wrongs?

Do I hate evil and rejoice in
truth?

Do I always protect, always
trust, always hope, always
persevere?

Do I fail?

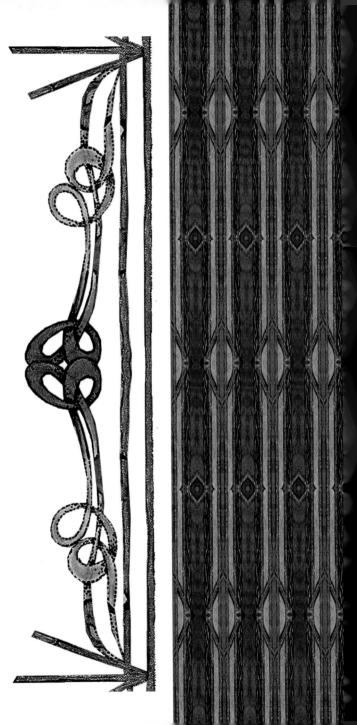

Prayer

Dear Lord,

Please help me to
love others and
the world around me -
even when
I'm hurting.

Please grant me
the grace to
accept the love
offered to me -
even when I am
feeling unworthy.

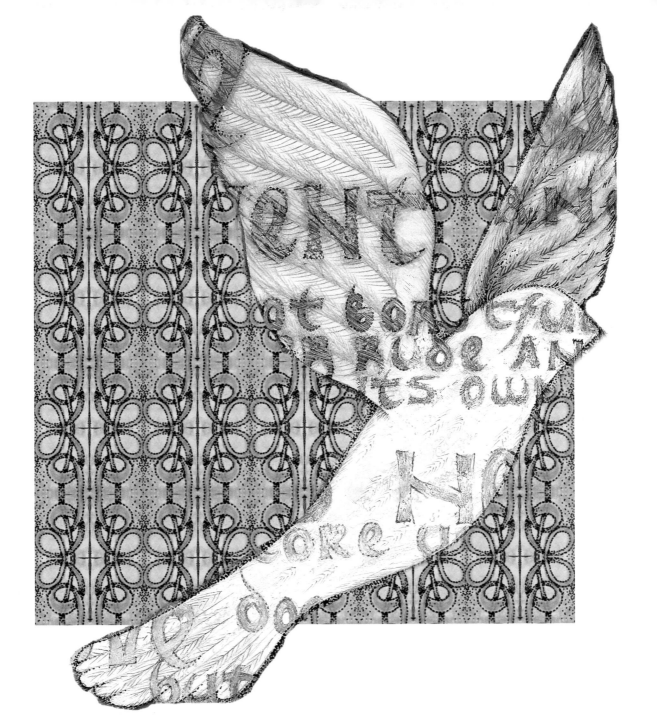

A Call to Hope

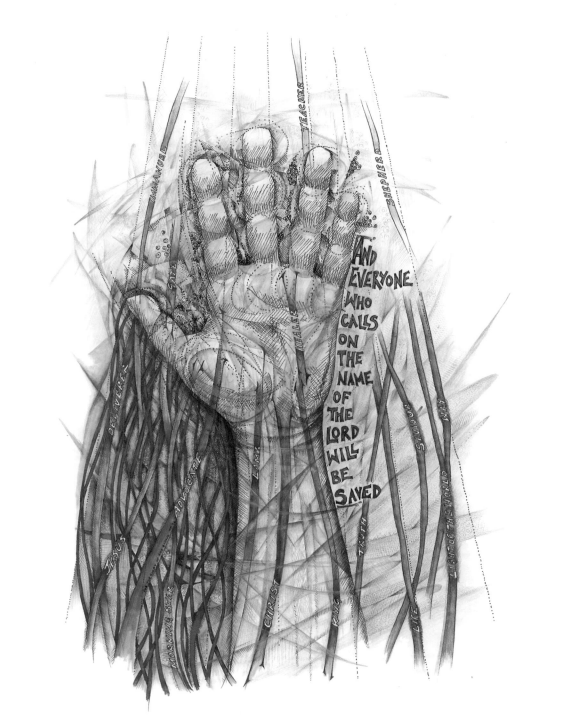

To reach out

Help me Dear Lord,
    to care too much,
    to love too freely,
    to pray unceasingly,
    to forgive endlessly,
    to laugh fearlessly,
    to question,
    to live,
    to be who I am,
    to be where I am,
    to be what I am,
    to hope,
    to believe,
    to reach out my hand.

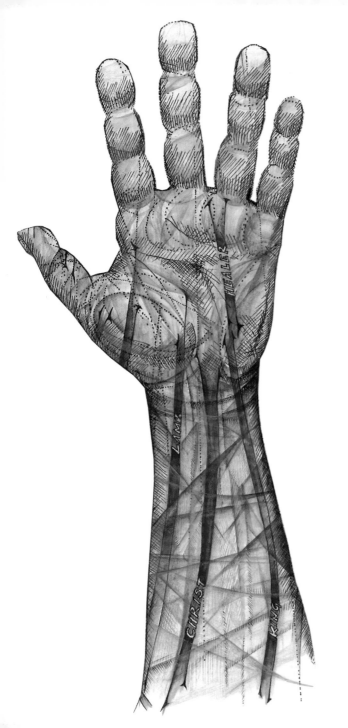

My Jesus

My Jesus, my Jesus, my Saviour, my Friend,
Hear my voice, hear my call.
It's not gone well today.

As the day winds down my mind spins around,
So much I don't understand,
So much I'm holding on to.
My Jesus, my Jesus, my Saviour, my Friend,
Hear my voice, hear my call.
It's not gone well today.

Please calm my anxious thoughts,
Help me to understand at least my part,
Help me to hold on to You.
My Jesus, my Jesus, my Saviour, my Friend,
Hear my voice, hear my call.
It's not gone well today,
I've struggled again.
May tomorrow be better, O Lord.

Meditation

I'm a terrible worrier, there, I've admitted it. I'm a Christian who trusts God and believes that He cares for me and yet I can worry for England, especially, but not only, when I'm over-tired or under the weather. When everything is going wrong I worry, when everything is going right I will look for something to worry about. I'm really rubbish at laying down those burdens, and when I do manage it, I usually pick them up again at a later date. You would think that because I worry I ask for divine help more often than someone who doesn't, that I would be used to calling on Jesus. Sadly the opposite is true. It's taken me years to realise that my worrying is a miserable, lonely, totally immersing occupation which leaves no room for rational thought or inclination for prayer.

Maybe it's because when we pray we can become particularly transparent to God. Asking Him to prevent 'things' from happening feels so silly when there are people who are in the midst of real suffering, and the globe is warming, and there is war. But prayer is a powerful thing, not only is it our way of communicating with our creator but it is also a way we can fight against the evils in the world we live in.

Turning worrying into praying is the only way forward for the person who doesn't want to remain bowed under the weight of everything that could go wrong. It's not a bad thing to recognise that life isn't always likely to go smoothly, it's not a bad thing to recognise dangers and potential problems, those are the things we can pray about. The letting go and leaving them with God, that's the hard bit. I have to keep reminding myself of a picture I once had where I was laying large stones at the foot of the cross, Jesus was on the cross but not nailed to it, he was radiant and held there as if by love alone. Each stone was a worry I had at that time. As the pile grew I found that I could climb the stones as though they were steps until I was so high I could look into Jesus' face. His eyes held all the love, acceptance and peace I was craving. Had I taken each stone worry back rather than leave it I would never have seen His smile.

He has given us reason to hope even when it's difficult not to worry about what the future may hold because He taught us that love conquers death, that each one of us is precious and that we can make a difference to the world we live in by treating others as we would like to be treated.

Design notes

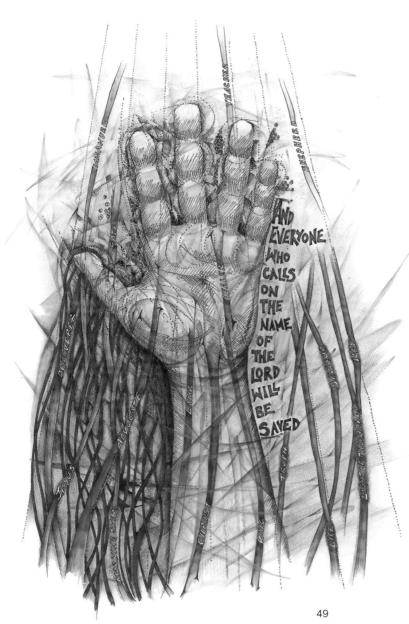

This piece woke me at four in the morning the day after being told about someone who was very ill.

She had seen something in a piece of artwork that reminded her of a relationship she once had with God and had begun to speak to Him again.

I woke from a dream where I saw a hand reaching upwards, it was a desperate and yet bold hand, hopeful and proud.

In my drawing I wanted to show the hand with God's life-blood flowing through it, feeding the body and drawing it closer.

Every large vein became a name of Jesus and therefore a call, our deepest cells calling out to their creator, wanting to return to safety through the blood.

Joel 2:32 And everyone who calls on the name of the LORD will be saved,

Gen. 4:26 At that time men began to call on the name of the LORD.

Try

In an increasingly mad world where minorities have the loudest voice, we are confronted by a media which chips away at the hope we need to live balanced lives. It can be helpful to know what triggers our own worry-buttons, is it reading the daily papers? Watching the news? Lack of sleep? Lack of space to just be? Maybe a combination. If you are a bit of a worrier, or even if you aren't try the following...

1. Have a news fast, 24 hours of no TV or radio news or papers. This is not running away from life or the reality of the world, it is giving you time to ask God what is really important for you to be concerned about at this time in your life.
2. Join an intercessory team or a prayer group, bring your worries out into the open with people you can trust and who will pray with you. Be aware that this is a group exercise and you will be praying for other's problems and worries, that in itself can be helpful.
3. Keep a prayer journal and record every personal worry alongside the good things to be thankful for and the prayers for others. Review the journal regularly and note when prayers are answered and worries resolved; if they are ongoing consider asking others to pray for you and with you.
4. Say out loud 'Jesus I need You, help me please'.
5. Worship, worship and more worship.

You will no doubt be wondering if these exercises actually work and whether or not I have used them to any effect. The answer is yes, they all work, but I am aware that I am an ongoing creation and I need to keep working at my weaknesses. God could make me different immediately so that I'd never worry, but I think He likes to meet us halfway sometimes, so that we learn from our striving and as we learn we can share our experiences with others.

Romans 10:12-13 For there is no difference between Jew and Gentile - the same Lord is Lord of all and richly blesses all who call on him, for, everyone who calls on the name of the LORD will be saved.

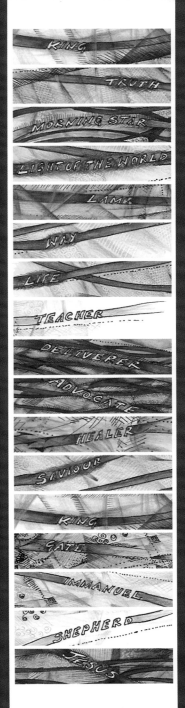

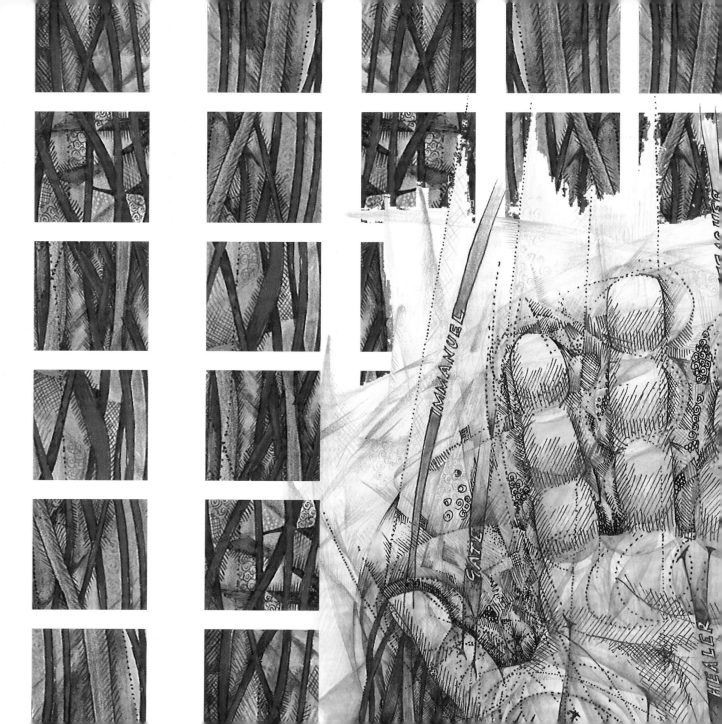

Prayer

Please Lord grant us the grace,
　　to change our hearts,
　　to open our minds.
　　　Grant us the grace,
　　to bless our small corner,
　　to encourage each other.
　　　Grant us the grace,
　　to pray for the world,
　　to care too much.
　　　Grant us the grace,
　　　please Lord.

A Call to Action

Glory to God in the highest and peace to His people on earth.

Something

We wait, and we wait
and we wait.
We wait
for peace.
And we tut and we sigh and we say
Why don't 'they' do 'something'?
As if 'they' were someone else,
And doing were the only option,
And 'something' were an answer.

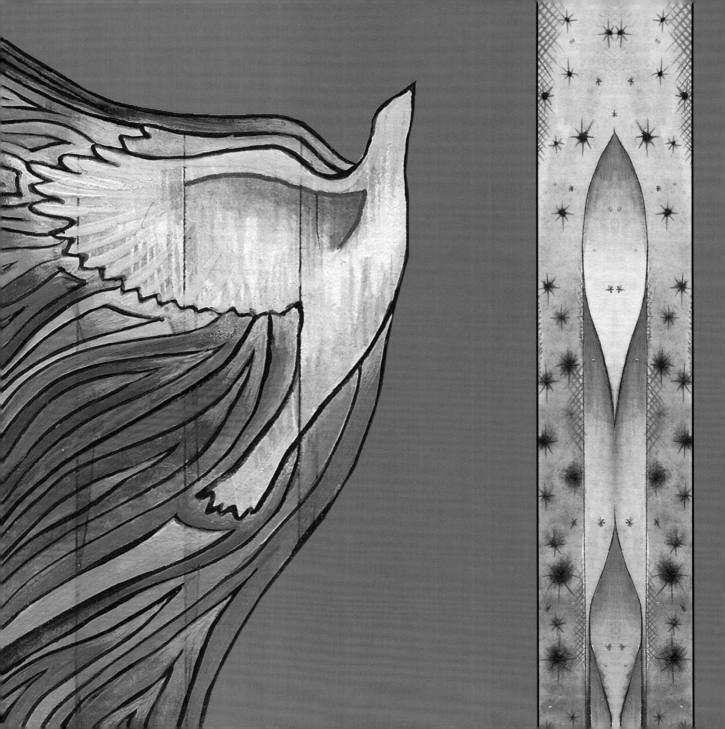

Luke 2:13-15

Suddenly a great company of the heavenly host appeared with the angel, praising God and saying, "Glory to God in the highest, and on earth peace to men on whom his favour rests." When the angels had left them and gone into heaven, the shepherds said to one another, "Let's go to Bethlehem and see this thing that has happened, which the Lord has told us about."

Design notes

This was a Christmas image which expresses Gods desire for us to enjoy peace in this world and reminding us that offering to God our unconditional worship, restoring the wonder, majesty and glory of the Godhead, is part of achieving that goal of peace.

The colours and lines of the background are reminiscent of the Aurora Borealis which we saw a few years ago over the Island, the colours were vivid reds and greens with golds, yellows and blues flickering against an inky black sky. We wondered if the record in the Anglo-Saxon Chronicle which says, "…immense flashes of lightning, and fiery dragons were seen flying in the air…" referred to a rare but brilliant display of the Aurora. We were amazed at the drama of the fiery sky and could easily imagine a less informed society attributing its source to dragons!

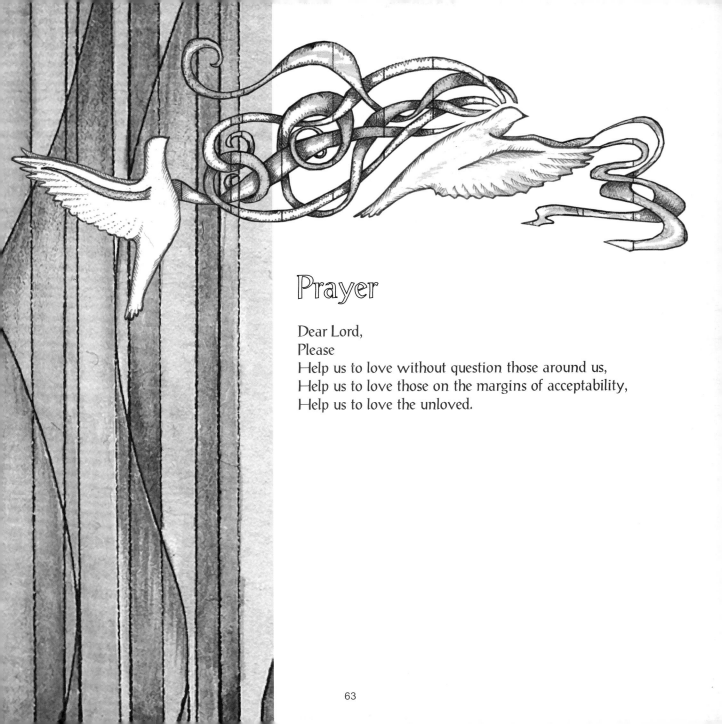

Prayer

Dear Lord,
Please
Help us to love without question those around us,
Help us to love those on the margins of acceptability,
Help us to love the unloved.

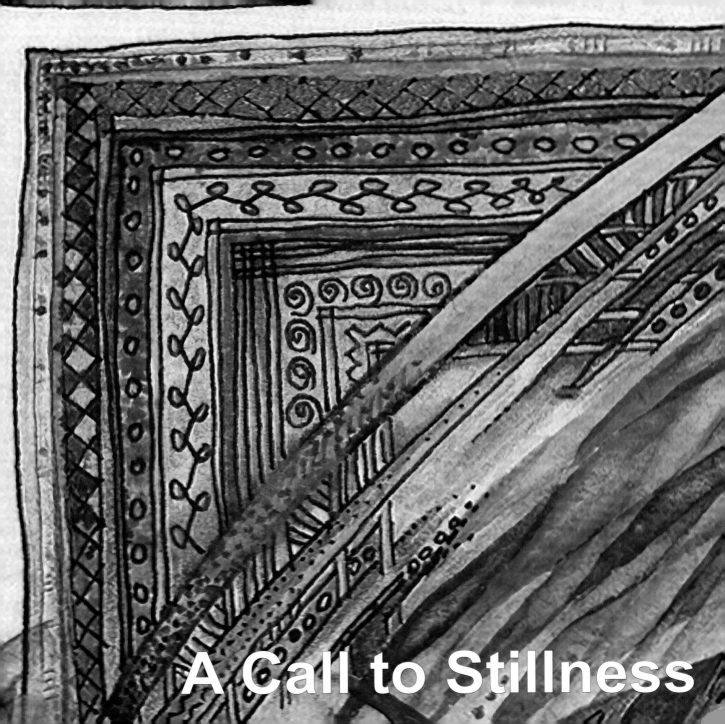
A Call to Stillness

Today

What's the rush? Sit a while.

He must be hungry,
They'll all be thirsty.

Peace beloved.
This is important, come and listen.

The house is a mess,
They're sitting on the floor!

Rest beloved.
There won't be another time like this.

Dirty cups, dirty plates,
What must they think?

Calm beloved.
For today I am here.

Today I will feed your soul.
Today I will comfort you.
Today My love is enough.
Today I am with you.

Pray Some More

I'm sorry I didn't catch that,
I'll just do this, and that, and that, and this.
Do unto others as - what?
As you would like a new shelf?
That sounds unlikely I'm sure.
But I must do this, and that, and that, and this.
I can't stop, too much to do today.
The kingdom of heaven's like a custard tree!
I just don`t believe in that sort of thing!
And I must do this, and that, and that, and this.
If I don't it'll all fall apart!

My Jesus I hear You.
I stop, I wait, I listen, I pray, I stay,
I'll try to be like You.
To be your eyes, Your ears, Your hands
And love others as You love me
I stop, I wait, I listen, I pray, I stay,
I want to see your kingdom
Established here on earth as on high
And I believe I can make a difference
So I stop, I wait, I listen, I pray, I stay,
And I pray some more.

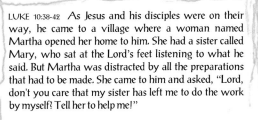

LUKE 10:38-42 As Jesus and his disciples were on their way, he came to a village where a woman named Martha opened her home to him. She had a sister called Mary, who sat at the Lord's feet listening to what he said. But Martha was distracted by all the preparations that had to be made. She came to him and asked, "Lord, don't you care that my sister has left me to do the work by myself? Tell her to help me!"

"Martha, Martha," the Lord answered, "you are worried and upset about many things, but only one thing is needed. Mary has chosen what is better, and it will not be taken away from her."

Mary has chosen what is better, and it will not be taken away from her.

Meditation

The story of Mary and Martha is not only about making the most of time with people and prioritising the important things of life, it is also about the true meaning of hospitality.

I tend to be a bit of a Martha. I would like to think that if Jesus stopped by for a cuppa I would stop what I was doing and be a Mary for a while, only thing is, would I recognise Him if He did? I believe that there is something of Christ in all of us and so when Auntie Mabel or Mr Smith visit is it like Jesus is sitting in your kitchen, munching your custard creams and telling you about their latest experiences at the supermarket? When Fred stays a bit longer than is polite is it Jesus you are hearing tell the same uninteresting story you've heard many times over?

Hospitality is not as simple as opening your home and being available to listen to people. True hospitality is about really caring about those people and the lives they are living. True hospitality is about giving up time to devote to others even when the washing is piling up and you've not had a moment to yourself for days – without complaining about it afterwards or feeling virtuous at having done a good deed.
True hospitality is about having a spirit humble and curious enough to learn from the Auntie Mabel and Freds of the world. True hospitality is about loving and praying.

Design notes

The idea behind this piece was to show Martha rushing around doing chores whilst Mary sat still at Jesus' feet. I used a technique of design which suggested a whirl of movement for Martha with a focus of plain, bright white at the centre to draw the eye to the tender moment when Jesus reaches out his hand towards Mary. This piece was really hard to finish as the stillness to work in the appropriate frame of mind eluded me for a long time. It's a piece which I feel I should see, absorb and heed every day!

Activity

We cannot physically sit at Jesus' feet but there are ways we can be in his presence, opening our hearts and minds in an attitude of hospitality to His presence. One of the ways we forge relationships with people is to find out as much as we can about their lives, their experiences, their views and their attitudes, it can be the same with Jesus today.

Using the Bible as your starting point discover as much as you can about the man Jesus and His Godhead. What did He say? What did others think about Him? What difference did He make to the lives of the people around Him?

Imagine yourself at key moments in Jesus' life.

Imagine what you might say to Him or ask Him if you were sitting side by side at supper.

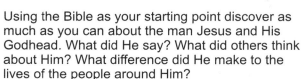

Prayer

At times I'm like Martha Lord,
so concerned about doing, getting things sorted
and making everything just right.
When I am able to be like Mary, Lord,
I usually feel guilty at the things I've left undone.
I pray for peace in the midst of the Martha times
and for renewal and inspiration in my Mary times.

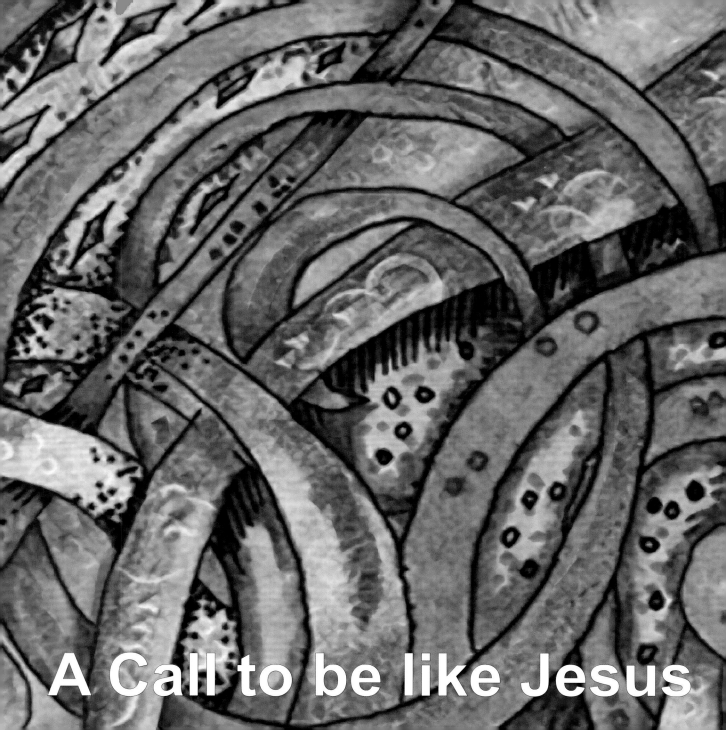

A Call to be like Jesus

Christ Be

Christ be at the centre of my mind and my heart,
Christ be at the centre of my thoughts and my words,
Christ be at the centre of my joy and my pain,
Christ be at the centre of my home and my journey,
Christ be at the centre of my peace and my turmoil,
Christ be my inspiration and my guide.

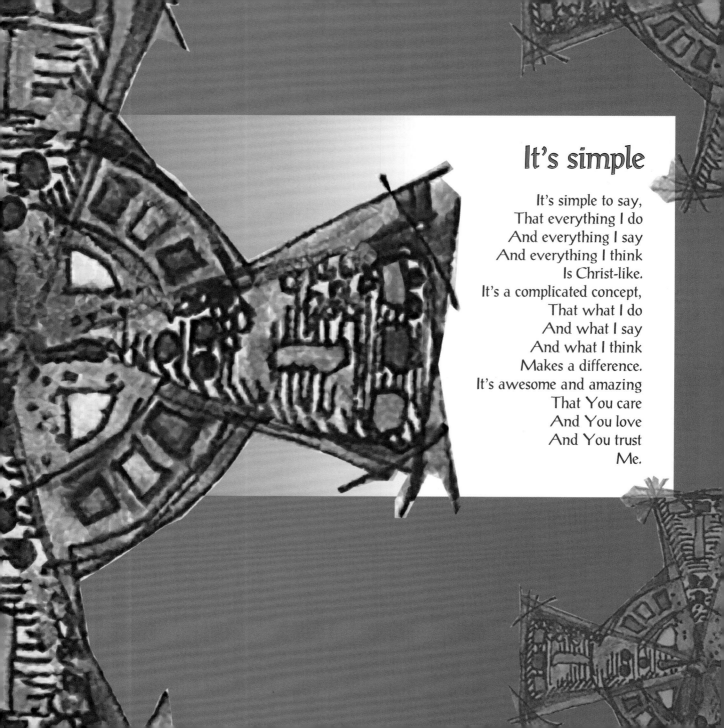

It's simple

It's simple to say,
That everything I do
And everything I say
And everything I think
Is Christ-like.
It's a complicated concept,
That what I do
And what I say
And what I think
Makes a difference.
It's awesome and amazing
That You care
And You love
And You trust
Me.

Meditation

Theresa of Avila left us a beautiful prayer, *Christ has no body now but yours*. The idea that we are entrusted by God to perceive the world as He does and act in response is an awesome and yet frightening idea. I can remember travelling on a bus in my student days, suddenly I saw every person around me as an individual loved passionately by God, the cuddly looking lady in the old-fashioned coat with her shopping bag on her knees and her wrinkly stockings, God loved her! The rough looking teenage lad with his home-done 'LOVE', 'HATE' tattoos and ripped, grubby jeans, God loved him. The old man muttering and dribbling slightly down his frayed overcoat, God loved him and in that moment, at about 4.20pm on a rainy weekday in March, I loved them all, because God showed me them through His eyes and each one was precious.

If I travelled much on buses nowadays I would probably crank up the mp3 player, plug in my headphones and bury my head in a good book, I'm really sad to admit that. It wasn't that I struck up any significant conversations on that particular journey, that moment of God-inspired love for my fellow man didn't remain so intense, but I did try to be open to conversations on my subsequent travels because I felt that people mattered to me because they mattered to God.

I don't go on buses nowadays and it takes more effort to be interested in strangers because life is so much more consumed by family and work, but the headphones won't be coming with me to the shops or for a walk so maybe some of those strangers will have the chance to become friends.

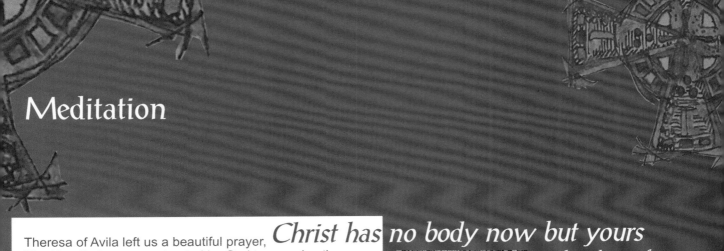

Christ has no body now but yours

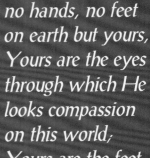

no hands, no feet
on earth but yours,
Yours are the eyes
through which He
looks compassion
on this world;
Yours are the feet
with which He
walks to do good;
Yours are the hands
with which He
blesses all the world.
Yours are the hands,
yours are the feet,
Yours are the eyes,
you are His body.
Christ has no body
now but yours.

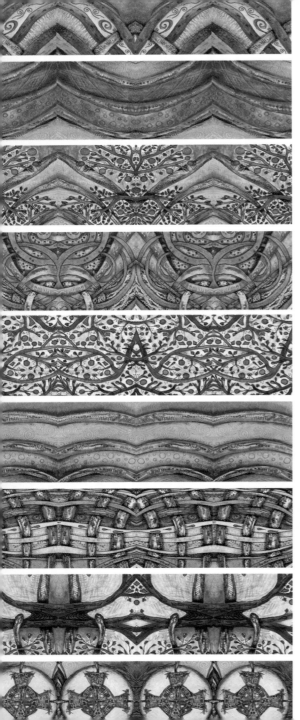

Design notes

This piece was the result of meditating on what defines a Christ-centred life. I wanted to show the fruitfulness that comes from a life rooted in the cross of Christ and the refreshment and cleansing available to us. In the spirals I wanted to express the vibrancy of a Christ-centred life and four aspects of life; birth, death, spirituality and growth.

Each arm of the spiral, each aspect of life, is cross hatched and bumpy with patches of light and dark, showing the erratic nature of living. Each arm ends but its outline turns back towards the cross, showing that everything came from God and returns to God.

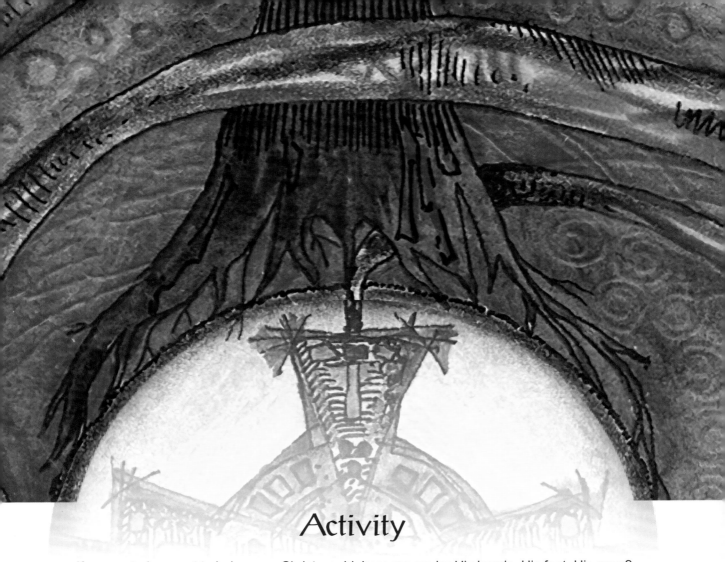

Activity

If we are truly meant to behave as Christ would, how can we be His hands, His feet, His eyes?
Consider the following questions:

Does doing what Jesus would do mean that we should put ourselves in uncomfortable or even dangerous situations?

If Jesus were here today how would He respond to some of the issues we confront today such as multi-culturalism, materialism, developing/western world contrasts, global warming and inequality?

Ask yourself "What am I doing that would please God, that would make Him proud of me?"

Matthew
10:31
So don't
be afraid;
you are
worth
more
than
many
sparrows.

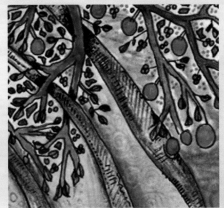

Prayer

Dear Lord,
Please take the fear from my heart
and replace it with Your love,
Please take the turmoil from my mind
and replace it with Your peace,
Please take the weariness from my body
and replace it with Your strength.

My Dear Ones

My dear ones, O God,
bless Thou and keep;
the homes of my dear ones, O God,
bless Thou and keep;
the dear ones of my dear ones, O God,
bless Thou and keep;
My dear ones, O God,
bless Thou and keep in every place where they are.
This night and tomorrow's day
and every night and day thereafter.

Family

More than Mum and Dad
Sister and Brother
Gran and Grandad
Aunt and Uncle
Niece and Nephew
Cousin Fred...
...Twice removed.
More than Wives and Husbands
However devoted,
More than Friends
However close.
They shape our life,
Our personality,
Our dreams.
But our Father all around us,
He shapes our soul.

MF 2006
FOR THE GLORY OF GOD ALONE

Meditation

The story of when Jesus introduced the disciple (John 19:26-27) to His mother, Mary, saying 'This is your son' has always made me think about the idea of 'Family' and what it means. Nowadays it's nothing exceptional to grow up with two or more fathers and multiple sets of grandparents, siblings with different parentage and children adopted from different countries and cultures.
The people we choose to live with or be surrounded by become our family. When I married I found myself with an extra Mum & Dad, grandparents, an Aunt and Uncle, a sister and brother and later a niece and two nephews. I also found myself with more family in the form of my husband's cousins and Fleeson family friends many of whom had been adopted as Aunts and Uncles over the years. All these people became family.

As human beings we are all related biologically in some distant way and as God's children we are family on a deeper, spiritual level. The concept is amazing, that the man who walks past your window every day is your brother, that well-known presenter on TV is your cousin, the small girl starving in Africa is your sister, the prostitute on the corner is family.

There's an old saying that 'You don't choose your family'. That holds true, the members of God's Family are scarily diverse because God accepts and loves and desires the Fatherhood of every single person on this planet. Every single one. If we recognise His role in our lives then we must accept all the brothers and sisters and aunts and uncles and cousins He has chosen for us, regardless of their circumstances.

Design notes

This was perhaps the most complicated piece I have done to date. For the first, and probably the only time, I used a heavily tweaked computer font for the wording, arranged using a software package which allowed me to change the sizing of the letters and place them in an interesting way whilst retaining the regularity of identical shaped letters and perfectly spaced, straight lines and borders.

I added to the arrangement of words very faint photographs and printed onto the heavyweight cartridge paper I usually use. The photographs gave me enough information to build dot impressions of the faces and buildings and the words provided the foundation for pattern and knotwork to be added.

Using the perfect regularity of the computer aided design meant that I could experiment with using a lot of words in a small space and the regularity contrasted beautifully with the freedom of the patterns.

PS 67:1 May God
be gracious to us
and bless us
and make
his face
shine
upon us

Activity

Consider:

What does accepting all people as
Family really mean in everyday life?

How does it change our world view to
see everyone as someone important and
precious to us personally?

How then should we treat our blood
family?

Prayer

Thank you for my family,
for the people who are close to me
emotionally,
spiritually,
physically.
I place each one in Your care.

A Call to Remember

BE STILL, LET THE TIDE OF MEM...
LISTEN TO THE WHISPERS OF T...
FEEL THE BREATH OF WIS...
RETURN TO
THE PLACE OF PEACE
YOUR HOLY ISLAND

Be Still

Be still,
let the tide of memories wash over you.
Listen to the whispers of the Saints,
Feel the breath of wisdom refresh your mind,
Return to the place of peace.
Your holy island.

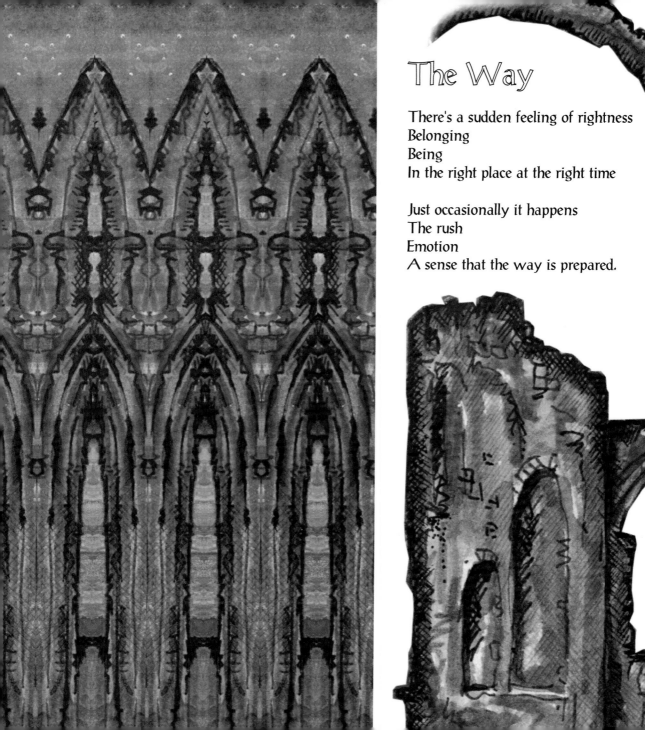

The Way

There's a sudden feeling of rightness
Belonging
Being
In the right place at the right time

Just occasionally it happens
The rush
Emotion
A sense that the way is prepared.

Meditation

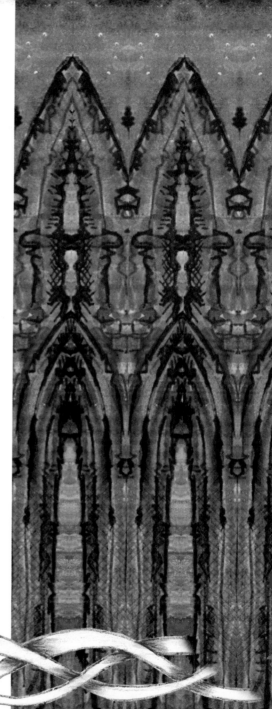

Memories are precious; anyone who has had the feeling that they have forgotten something important they know they should remember is aware of just how important they are. Good memories transport us to a happy place where friends we have lost live again and places which have changed beyond recognition are restored to a sunny glow. Embarrassing memories, or as a friend of mine used to call them, 'cringes', can be useful in helping us to understand ourselves, our motives and our weaknesses. Even bad memories may help us to grow emotionally and spiritually, if we allow them to.

Finding a special place to go to in real life can be restoring, rediscovering that special place in our imagination may be even more helpful especially as cost and time are no limitation. My special place is in Cornwall, (that's not to say I don't love and appreciate Holy Island but even if you live in a wonderful place it's good to have somewhere else to go to recharge); it has lovely sandy beaches, hundreds of artists, dramatic seas and a serenity that survives even August crowds. I can walk its narrow streets in my mind, hear the gulls and the waves, smell the spray and feel the sand between my toes. I spent many childhood holidays there and as an adult manage to return every few years. Even holidays there which have been spoilt by rain or problems of a more human kind cannot diminish the memories I have.

For many, Lindisfarne is that special place, it is steeped in prayer, fiercely Northumbrian and uniquely beautiful. It teaches many lessons to a hurried and secular world, its lonely beaches can speak of calm and time to just be; its history tells of a triumph of faith over terror, the Island has retained a Christian presence despite it's monastery being repeatedly destroyed; its wildlife communicates transience and yet also stability as migrating birds return to visit year after year; the village represents a diverse community of many different sorts of people and the causeway may be symbolic of leaving the known world behind and then returning to it refreshed.

It is easy to get tied up in the strings of everyday life, the hum-drum, the stress, the sameness, the weariness and that is why a place and time apart is so important in restoring a balance. Refreshing the spirit and the mind with memories of somewhere different, allowing God to meet and talk with you on your quiet beach or forest walk is a way of defying the draining demands of modern life and saying to God, "Meet with me, let's spend some time together, just You and me".

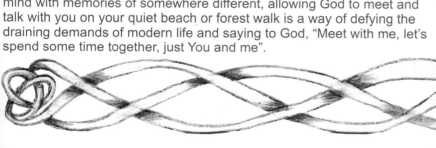

Design notes

The Holy Island piece is collage-like in construction, it depicts scenes from around the Island of Lindisfarne combined with images from the Lindisfarne Gospels and the poem itself.

BE STILL   LET THE TIDE OF MEMORIES WASH OVER YOU
LISTEN TO THE WHISPERS OF THE SAINTS
FEEL THE BREATH OF WISDOM REFRESH YOUR MIND
RETURN TO
THE PLACE OF PEACE
YOUR HOLY ISLAND

JOHN 14:25-27 "All this I have spoken while still with you. But the Counsellor, the Holy Spirit, whom the Father will send in my name, will teach you all things and will remind you of everything I have said to you. Peace I leave with you; my peace I give you. I do not give to you as the world gives. Do not let your hearts be troubled and do not be afraid."

Activity

Wherever your special place is the memories of it should be nurtured. Even if you will never return physically keep it fresh in your mind by regular 'visits'. I remember reading a novel once where an elderly housebound character kept scrapbooks of places she'd never been. She would plan itineraries and in her mind visit all the places on the pages, meet the locals, eat the food and return 'home' with tales of adventures. In the novel the activity was seen as being just rather sad and yet wouldn't it be wonderful to give ourselves permission to imagine, to daydream in the way we did as children.

Schedule a meeting with God, if your life is busy you may find you need to pencil in time to meet with friends so do the same with God.

Create a visual journal about your special place, it could include photographs and sketches and your thoughts about what makes it your special haven.

Prayer

Dear Lord,

May my special place be filled with your
presence that others might be refreshed,

May my spirit be restored so that I might
share Your peace.

Amen

A Call to Completeness

I Believe

I believe that there is nothing in death or life
that can separate us from the love of God,
Nothing in the realms of the unseen
that can separate us from the love of God,
Nothing in the world as it is or shall be
that can separate us from the love of God,
Nothing in the natural forces of the universe
that can separate us from the love of God,
Nothing above or below
that can separate us from the love of God,
Nothing in all creation
that can separate us from the love of God,
Which is ours through Jesus Christ our Lord.

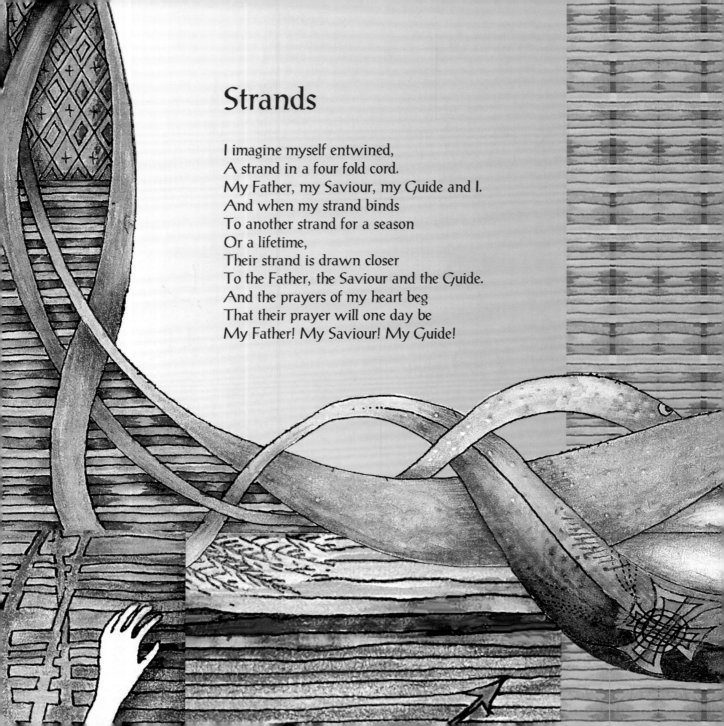

Strands

I imagine myself entwined,
A strand in a four fold cord.
My Father, my Saviour, my Guide and I.
And when my strand binds
To another strand for a season
Or a lifetime,
Their strand is drawn closer
To the Father, the Saviour and the Guide.
And the prayers of my heart beg
That their prayer will one day be
My Father! My Saviour! My Guide!

Romans 8:38-39 For I am **convinced** that **neither** **death** nor life, neither **angels** nor **demons**, neither **the present nor the future**, nor **any** **powers**, neither **height** nor **depth**, nor **anything else** in all creation, will be able to separate us from **the love of God** that is in **Christ Jesus our Lord**.

Meditation

It is amazing to think that because of one action two thousand years ago we can live knowing that we need never be separated from our creator God. Even in the simple day to day actions of living, God is there, right beside us. <u>Nothing</u> can separate us.

There are times however when it feels as though we are alone, all sense of purpose and faith is lost and we feel adrift, abandoned and powerless. These are the desert times when God may allow us to feel that way for a while for a purpose. It could be that life has been going well and relying on God has seemed less necessary and the conversations He loves to have with us have diminished to cursory nods and waves. Then suddenly we feel bereft, God has gone! Left us alone in the big, bad world and we don't know what to do. God might not jump in at that point with a booming voice or a flashing light and make everything OK again. He might just leave us to re-learn how to pray, how to listen and how to obey.

He hasn't really gone away, He never left.

Design notes

I enjoyed illustrating the individual aspects of this powerful statement, look out for hands reaching from above and below, the time-line from creation to the future, the strand of DNA...all reinforced with the hands spread in supplication and awe at the amazing declaration.

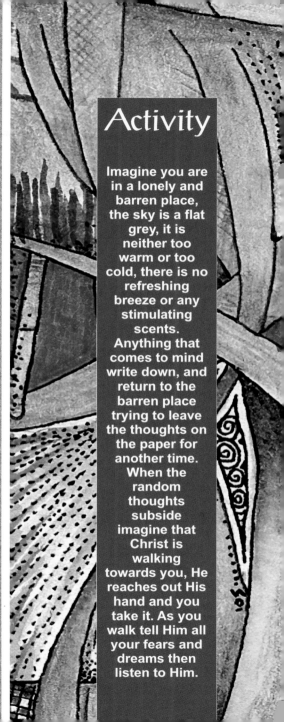

Activity

Imagine you are in a lonely and barren place, the sky is a flat grey, it is neither too warm or too cold, there is no refreshing breeze or any stimulating scents. Anything that comes to mind write down, and return to the barren place trying to leave the thoughts on the paper for another time. When the random thoughts subside imagine that Christ is walking towards you, He reaches out His hand and you take it. As you walk tell Him all your fears and dreams then listen to Him.

2 Corinthians 13:14

May the grace of the Lord Jesus Christ, and the love of God, and the fellowship of the Holy Spirit be with you all.

Romans 5:1

Therefore, since we have been justified through faith, we have peace with God through our Lord Jesus Christ.

1 John 4:9

This is how God showed his love among us: He sent his one and only Son into the world that we might live through him.

Luke 18:27

Jesus replied,

"What is impossible with men is possible with God."

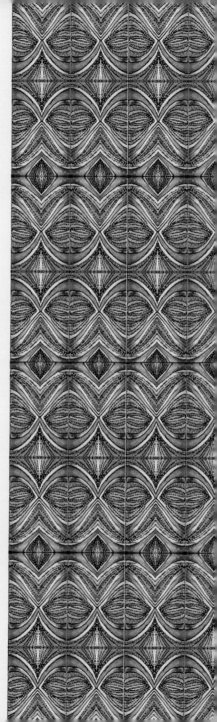

Prayer

I believe that your presence
Is my strength,
My hope
My purpose,
I believe in the love
That conquers death,
Defeats evil
And is life,
I believe in the joy
That is deep,
That cleanses
That heals.
I believe that You are here
Beside me,
Around me
Holding me.

A Call to Creativity

A Trying Time

Woven cords of gifting, In the ebb and flow of trying,
Flexing - Passions re-igniting, stirring, shaping, burning, waiting.

Examples of the men of then, made new in the now.
Future seen in the light of the past, vessels filled.
Carpet patterns speaking.
A time of making, sowing - refreshment flowing.
Cleansing, kneeling, hoping, knowing.

Some people

Some people say
That they
Aren't arty
Or creative
But they live
Amidst beauty
They can bake
They will take
Time to garden
Or decorate
And titivate
Their homes
They can storytell
Entertain well
Sing a note or two
So when they say
That they
Aren't arty
It's just not true!

Meditation

One of the saddest things I heard in the context of creativity was a young man commenting that he just didn't 'get' art. Nothing artistic had ever engaged him and he had closed his mind to the possibility that something might. His comment stayed with me like an itch, niggling away somewhere unreachable. It challenged me to realise that not everyone sees the world the same way, not everyone can see God in art.

But why can't they engage with it? I have met many people who tell me that they are not artistic and yet they can appreciate art, people who were told at school to choose science over art who, despite having not lifted a paintbrush since, are inspired by it. If I want to convince someone that art is important, and more significantly, a way of seeing and meeting God, what can I say? How can I prove it?

I suppose the first thing would be to explain that the purpose of art is to challenge our preconceived ideas, to challenge our view of the world we live in and to enrich our lives with colour and beauty; a piece of art may do all three things but will often only do one or two. The next thing would be to give them a pencil and pad and lead them through exercises which would aim to reawaken the inner child who loves to grab a crayon and just make marks on the paper, simple delight in the ability to create a unique image with no ulterior motive or need for an end result, just enjoyment of the action. Then give them room to experiment, to play and have fun with materials, again with no need to produce anything other than textures, colours and marks. The next stage would be to encourage them to allow God to speak through the action, to invite Him to speak through the playing and the freedom of not needing to achieve, allow Him to heal by using the marks and colours to be an outward representation of inner emotions and thoughts.

Those ideas may be a starting point for the young man I mentioned, if he would be willing to be led into trying. Anyone who is told that they aren't good at something, will quickly lose any spark of interest they may have had and will lose an opportunity to meet God in a new way or have Him show them something about life through that medium. Obviously we're not all going to be experts in every field but regardless of the fruits of our trying it isn't the end result that matters it's the process itself and what it teaches you.

I will never be an Olympic swimmer but if I had never learnt to swim (and it took me a long time) I would never have experienced the peace of swimming down by the causeway when the tide was in or the fun of kayaking on a lake. The learning process itself was difficult but it taught me to persevere and that trying was just as important as succeeding.

Design notes

Woven Cords was written during an Arts Retreat several years ago. I wanted to illuminate the words of the poem in a more random way than usual to express the creative way that ideas flowed during the week and to have them focusing on a glowing sun which represented God's powerful inspiration and presence. I used areas of knotwork to express the community of people who met that week and to remind me of how we inspired each other, our lives crossing for a short while, weaving into each other's life fabric a new colour or texture.

Activity

Set aside an hour every so often, maybe when you're on holiday or on retreat, to play with art.

Without aiming for an end result just make marks on paper to see what happens or thread beads for the therapeutic effect of the repetitive action or knit for the pleasure of seeing the colours merge and the fabric be created.

Do anything creative but don't give it a purpose.

Where has your mind wandered during this process?

Lift the thoughts to God and ask for His blessing on them.

Look at what you have created and ask for His blessing on the work of your hands.

Bless the work

of our hands, O Lord

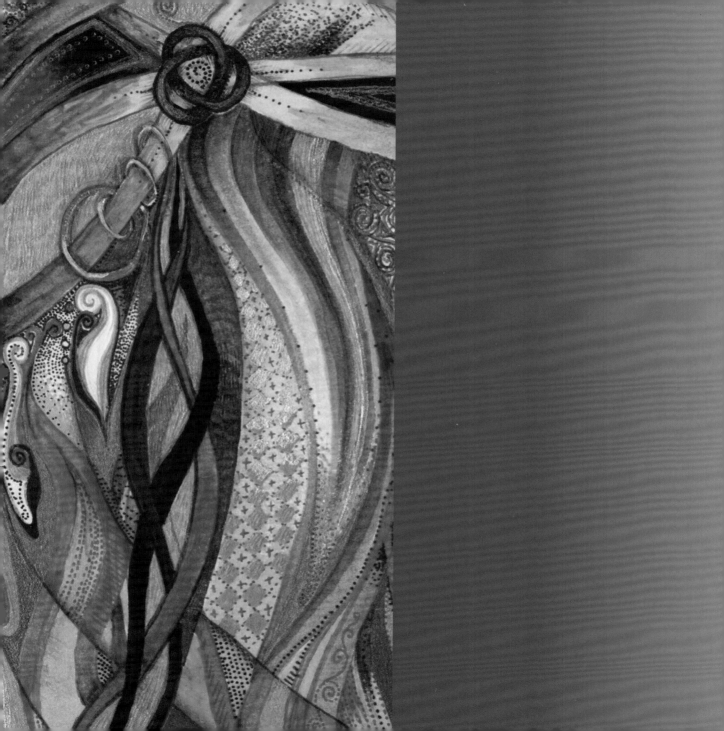

Prayer

Take the skills I have Lord,
And make them Your own.
Take the gifts I have
And bless their use,
Grant me opportunities
To try new things
And the courage
To make a mess of them.

Send us out

Send us out in the power of Your Spirit
to live and work to your praise and glory.

127

In Your Power

From the place where we are,
From the path we are following,
Send us out.

From our family and friends,
From our neighbours and community,
Send us out.

Into the hard places,
The untrodden paths,
In Your power.

Into company with the enemy,
The hostile lands,
In Your power.

Meditation

'Send us out in the power of Your Spirit to live and work to your praise and glory', these words have always reminded me why I do what I do, how I do it and when... because I am empowered to do so by the Spirit and because I want to give glory to God; in the strength of the Spirit and every moment of every day for the rest of my life.

Christian life is a daily call to be prepared to go where He wants us to and do what He wants us to. There is nothing that He requires us to do that He wasn't prepared to do when He walked on earth as a human and with the help and guidance of the Holy Spirit there is nothing that we cannot do in His name.

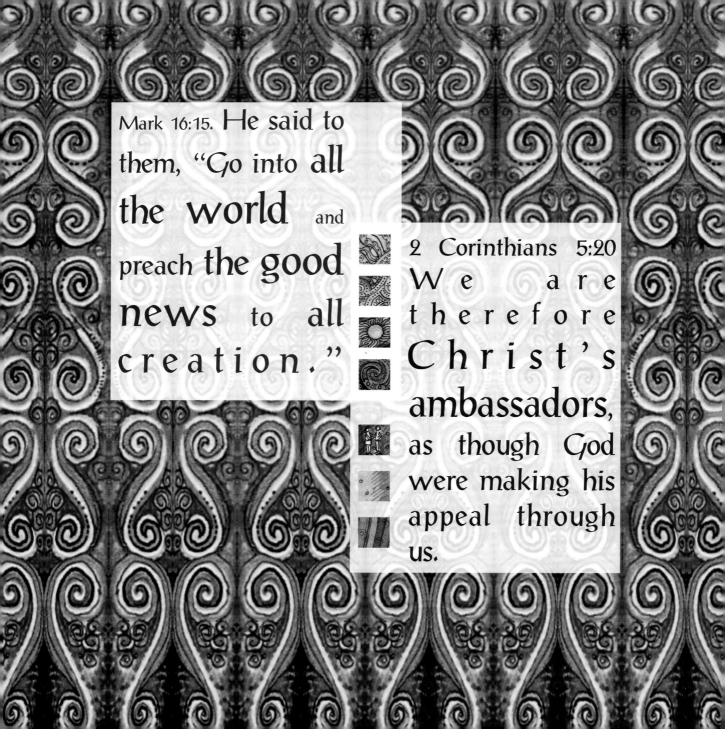

Mark 16:15. He said to them, "Go into all the world and preach the good news to all creation."

2 Corinthians 5:20 We are therefore Christ's ambassadors, as though God were making his appeal through us.

Design notes

'Send us Out' was lovely to work on, I tried to depict everyday street scenes and a variety of characters each travelling their life paths. All the paths leave the page to suggest that those travelling are able to go out into the world from their home environment.

I also included the imagery of hard roads to travel and activities like holidays and work.

Knotwork intersperses the whole piece reminding us of how our lives weave together to create the exciting patterns of life.

SEND US OUT IN THE POWER OF YOUR SPIRIT TO LIVE AND WORK TO YOUR PRAISE AND GLORY

Prayer

Today I pray
For those who have been called
To foreign lands and distant shores.
Lord, hear my prayer.

Today I pray
For those who have been called
Away from family and friends.
Lord, hear my prayer.

Today I pray
For those stuck in sameness
No escape, nothing new.
Lord, hear my prayer.

Today I pray
For those who listen for Him
Who wait for His direction.
Lord, hear my prayer.

Today I pray
For those who pray for others
May they be blessed.
Lord, hear my prayer.